ABOUT FACES

Positive stories of impactful people who have helped pivot my life.

By

Laurie Jankower James

Table of Contents

Foreword

My role models? Picture them as the unicorns of unconventional thinking – as rare and delightfully unusual as spotting a penguin in the desert. Even if some were blissfully unaware that they were guiding the ship of my life, their impact has set the trajectory of my very core into motion.

This book is my heartfelt standing ovation to all those accidental life coaches who unknowingly crafted me into the one-of-a-kind human being I am today. A toast to you, the unsung heroes of my escapade – you've wielded more influence than you'll ever know.

Through your guidance, I've embarked on a mission to prove that life is a carnival best enjoyed with a generous sprinkle of humor and dorkiness. Thanks for being the GPS of my life, guiding me through the maze of existence with the finesse of a tap-dancing flamingo. Buckle up because this adrenaline rush will take detours into amusing and truly bizarre realms!

Mervine L. Jankower (aka Dad): Dad always harbored a long-standing desire to write a book. Unfortunately, he never found the time because of his focused dedication to assisting others. This book pays tribute to his beautiful spirit, manifested through a passion for fostering open lines of communication within our family, our friends, and specifically to anyone who needed a listening ear.

Marilyn D. Jankower (aka Mom): The most self-actualized, talented, and bull-headed woman I've ever known. Mom's such a force of nature that I immediately morph into Ethel Mertz when she walks into a room! Her unwavering commitment to embracing individuality was pivotal in shaping me into the persistent, meticulous, and strong-willed person I am today. While many of her lessons were challenging *(to say the least),* each one contributed to developing my resilience by fearlessly doing the right thing in every situation.

Kenneth David James (aka Kenny): The heartbeat of my existence, who not only sees but embraces every quirk and curve of my being with pure love. Kenny is a gem in a sea of pebbles, an unsung hero whose mere presence ignites my soul. He's the catalyst for my authenticity, nudging me to be unapologetically myself in every endeavor. Infusing his world with joy is my calling as we weave our tapestry of life's shared moments, echoing our "Making Memories of Us" wedding song by Keith Urban.

Each chapter's title contains a "FACE" reference to carry on the book's theme. The tone used throughout is specifically meant to be humorous and conversational. The comfortable language should give a relaxed atmosphere for engagement and reflection.

1

Face To Face

'Watching one of the greatest love stories unfold right before me'

My parent's love story is an inspirational script waiting to be written. Mervine Jankower, the unsuspecting hero, stumbles into the scene when his roommate, Milton, is about to commit the literary crime of breaking up with Marilyn Davis via a disastrous Dear John letter.

Mervine, the confident literary superhero, swoops in with a "hold my beer" attitude, proclaiming, *"This is the worst letter I've ever seen. You can't send that to break up with anyone! I'll help you write something a bit more suitable."*

So, there's Mervine, gazing at Marilyn's photo for a bit of 'inspiration.' With careful finesse, he transforms the breakup letter into a poetic masterpiece.

He doesn't realize Marilyn's response would be laughter, as she had already lost interest in Milton and moved on.

Fast forward several months to a New Orleans fraternity weekend social. Mervine, already a Tulane law student, armed with Milton's permission *(who had moved to greener pastures, probably with a better ghostwriter),* invites Marilyn to New Orleans for the social. Sparks fly, but not without Mervine thinking Marilyn is a flirt, while she believes him to be full of himself. They are both right, of course. This classic meet-cute will turn into a love-at-first-sight triumph.

Ultimately, they both realize there's more to their encounter than meets the judgmental eye. Mervine declares Marilyn the smartest woman he's ever met, probably because she sees through his *"I'm too cool for school"* façade. And just like that, they are married in a mere 18 months. Cue the wedding bells and the obligatory romantic montage set to a '50s soundtrack.

Their early married life? Enchanting, of course. Dad handsomely sports an Air Force uniform while Mom takes charge as the CEO of their military household, and boom, baby boom – my brother arrives in 1957, while I make a grand entrance four years later. Let the Jankower family drama begin.

We live in Midland, Texas, a topography void of trees, just tumbleweeds, and a solid place for Dad to start putting that Tulane law degree to use. Crucial oil and gas industry connections are made there *(no doubt involving cowboy hats and oil barons).* After Dad receives an expected call asking for his Louisiana return to help run Mervine Kahn Company, the family business, they pack up and move us back to Louisiana and quickly settle into their newly constructed forever home.

Meanwhile, Mom ventures into teaching, opting for the flexibility of substitute teaching over a full-time role to harness the creativity needed to teach various subjects while raising two small children. Her commitment to students shows in her passionate and unwavering efforts. At several local high schools, she becomes the go-to for struggling students, privately tutoring Spanish with humor and warmth. Mom's genuine and disarming approach makes her memorable to each pupil. Raised by parents who encouraged embracing all life had to offer, Mom and Dad both relish attending local sports events and welcoming countless high school students into our home. They taught us that helping others is a calling.

Tipping a Hat to the Parental Predecessors: Mom's parents, Herbert and Bea, tied the knot in impromptu fashion at another couple's wedding, armed with a cigar band for a ring – an unconventional and budget-friendly touch if there ever was one. Dad's parents, Edel and Myrtis, eloped and then continued living separately with their respective parents to conceal the secret marriage for half a year, fearing parental disapproval, a clandestine courtship for the ages. (In case you're wondering, there was no hanky-panky, and their first child wasn't born until four years later!)

So, whether crafting your love story or just living vicariously through my parents' rom-com-worthy antics, remember: life's possibilities make the journey worthwhile, especially when it involves rewriting breakup letters and turning them into love notes.

2

Putting on a Game Face

'Growing up in a houseful of athletes'

Growing up in our house was like living in a sports-themed circus where our parents were the ringleaders. Weekends weren't just for relaxation; they were a showcase of college and professional athletes parading through our home.

Mom's formative years in San Antonio, Texas were a whirlwind of adventure, from marveling at Golden Gloves boxing matches to cheering on San Antonio's minor league baseball games, to enjoying musical events *(from Broadway to opera)*, and fearlessly ice skating at a local rink. Her parents were on a mission to mold well-rounded children, and they succeeded.

On the other hand *(pun intended)*, Dad, the ambidextrous marvel of athleticism, grew up in Rayne, Louisiana, where he seemed to have a hand in every sport imaginable. From football to basketball to baseball to golf, he dabbled with finesse, turning his childhood into a sporting smorgasbord. The home Mom and Dad created naturally became a melting pot of athletes filled with talent and knee braces.

Enter Ross Brupbacher, a high school senior who was undoubtedly the best-looking and most popular male on campus. Juggling school, sports, and family chores, Ross elevated multitasking to Olympic levels. Mom, who also taught at Ross's high school, saw him as the Hercules of academics and athletics combined. Ross was an All-American Athlete who graduated with multiple football scholarship offers. My parents celebrated his decision to attend Texas A&M by transforming our home into a mini-Texas A&M annex. Throughout Ross's four-year stint at A&M, our home became a pigskin palace, a collegiate gridiron gala event space. Teammates like Edd Hargett joined the party *(little did we know, he would later step in as a quarterback for the New Orleans Saints).*

Our living room blossomed into an NFL dream incubator. *(And yes, I opted for Mom's bathroom because our upstairs loo had turned into a makeshift locker room. Trading spitballs for sweaty jerseys wasn't exactly primary-school chic.)*

Larry Stegent, an A&M teammate of Ross', was another fixture in our home. The St. Louis Cardinals selected him in the first round of the 1970 NFL draft (8th overall), and he brought a vibrant and hilarious personality to our home despite facing a career-ending injury.

Doug Brodhead, *(an A&M Track & Field Hall of Famer),* Curley Hallman, *(a future Head Football Coach for LSU),* and Billy Bob Barnett, *(founder of Texas' iconic Billy Bob's in 1981 – at that time the world's largest honky-tonk bar and entertainment center),* all became honorary family members. Our home felt like a gathering hub for extraordinary sports legends to convene.

After graduating from A&M, the Chicago Bears drafted Ross, turning our living room into a pro football VIP lounge. When he returned home after a brutal rookie season, I nonchalantly greeted him at our front door, teasingly remarking, *"Oh, it's just Ross."* His response? A bear hug befitting a Chicago Bear, proving that even the NFL couldn't toughen him entirely.

At a Chicago Bears vs. Houston Oilers game, we met Ross' teammates Gale Sayers and Dick Butkus. Little did I know then the impact of those famed encounters; I was just a 10-year-old caught up in the excitement.

The University of Southwestern Louisiana (USL), our local college, introduced many athletes and bigger-than-life characters to our sitcom. Ragin' Cajun Basketball Coach and Hall of Famer Bobby Paschal became Dad's best friend, and Rich Sheubrooks, a Converse shoe sales guru-turned-sports mogul, was a great supporting cast member. Rich even arranged a surprise visit from Larry Bird's high school basketball coach, adding to the series' unpredictable charm. Such spontaneous events became a staple of our family's dynamic.

Recognizing my knack for communication, Rich played a pivotal role in launching my career in motivational and public speaking. It's a testament to life's unexpected turns; who could have predicted meeting a shoe salesman would have such a profound impact?

Side Note: Mom, our family's very own Yenta, boasted matchmaking skills that could make St. Valentine himself take notes. With instincts sharper than Cupid's arrows, her pairings often ignited a love as timeless as the cosmos. Consequently, earning her blessing became a sought-after rite of passage for all who relished her company.

Life Lesson: Growing up surrounded by these athletes significantly influenced my outlook, revealing the community impact and human nature transcending the boundaries of the field, court, course, pool, or track. This realization has enriched my personal and professional life, establishing connections with my husband's sports-centric interests while guiding student-athletes in the transitional period of navigating life after college. The valuable lessons gleaned from these athletes, as they confronted personal challenges and left enduring legacies, have instilled in me a deep understanding of the competition inherent in life and the pursuit of one's true calling.

In every facet of life, we engage in some form of competition. Translating the skills honed from these experiences into one's career journey can be the initial step toward identifying and fulfilling one's purpose. Each athlete who graced our home during my upbringing left an indelible mark on the world, a testament to their inspiring resilience in the face of personal challenges and propelling them toward the finish line of their unique journeys.

3

A Friendly Face

'Recognizing the people that God puts in our lives!'

Remember that middle school best friend who was your ride-or-die, who had your back through thick and thin? Mine happened to be Karen Reeves, the kindest and most beautiful friend I could ask for. With our birthdays just three days apart, we always shared a special bond. Our journey began in the chaotic world of 5th-grade band class – because nothing says *"friendship"* like learning how to toot on a clarinet together.

Our band director, Mr. John Zerangue, was a musical wizard. He could turn even the most tone-deaf among us into enthusiastic musicians. While not my instrument of choice, I begrudgingly picked up the clarinet. My supporter and giggle buddy Karen made the whole experience a riot.

Enthusiastically following the rules and possessing a fun sense of humor, she was the perfect accomplice in this symphonic adventure. Competing in weekly skills competitions, Karen always seemed to nab the chair just one spot ahead of me. The silver lining was spending a whole week sitting next to her.

Unable to talk during class, we became fluent in the sign language alphabet, much to our teacher's amusement. We knew a lifelong friendship was in the make – a silent, hilarious, clarinet-filled friendship.

Fast forward to high school, we took different paths, but we stayed in touch. Reuniting during sorority rush week, fate played its hand once again. Making a pact to keep our choices secret, we ultimately pledged the same sorority – Chi Omega! Our leadership teamwork was unparalleled as we rocked each role, from pledge class officers to participants in rush skits. We broke the sorority belief barrier by leading the charge to earn that coveted homecoming sweepstakes trophy together. Teamwork, baby!

Our junior year was a blast – Karen was the pledge trainer, and I served as chapter secretary. We graduated side by side, Karen married, and I stood beside her as a bridesmaid. When my big day arrived, she returned the favor as my matron of honor.

Life's up-and-down adventures continue, and friendships evolve, but Karen has been my constant. We've been each other's rock, from graduations to weddings to vacationing to all the ups and downs that come with life. Amazingly, we've never even argued. Now that's friendship! Our bond is unbreakable, proving that true friendships withstand the test of time.

Pivot: Approaching the grand milestone of turning 30 revealed an unexpected and beautiful opportunity for us. Unbeknownst to the other, we both enrolled in classes to become baptized. Despite being in different locations, our ceremonies synchronized perfectly. Now, we joyfully celebrate our church birthdays on the same day – talk about holy camaraderie!

So, who's your BFF on this crazy ride called life? Your sidekick, your confidante? If they're still kicking, grab a coffee with them. If they're not around, consider honoring their memory by infusing kindness into the world. Because even in the afterlife, I'm sure they'd appreciate a good laugh. Here's a toast to friendship, inside jokes, and sharing experiences that last a lifetime!

4

The Mirror Has Two Faces

'Weaving comedy and tragedy with excellent communication to help others'

Picture it: This wide-eyed junior high student was thrust into the unpredictable world of speech and debate – all thanks to the well-intentioned plotting of my parents. Convinced of the transformative magic of effective communication, my folks ingeniously enrolled me in the National Forensic League *(the "other" NFL).* Much to my surprise, they had my future all mapped out, with the ultimate destination in the lair of the formidable Novalyne Price Ellis, speech and debate coach extraordinaire.

Enter the whimsical world of Mrs. Ellis, the maverick mentor who defied convention by thrusting 8th graders into the cutthroat realm of high school speech tournament competitions. Behold the genius behind this pairing: two junior high students tackling *"The World of Carl Sandburg"* with a clumsy effort of interpretive dance, courtesy of Mrs. Ellis's unconventional brilliance. Imagine my partner and me - two clueless young girls - trying to make sense of Carl Sandburg's poetry and prose at such a young age.

While we may not have clinched any awards, our toolboxes became filled with the unique experience only dancing to Carl Sandburg could provide.

Transitioning into our freshman year, our duet partnership evolved into the realm of debate. I took charge of the dramatic expressive aspect of our team, complemented by my partner's superior debating skills with her research-heavy focus on facts, forming a formidable alliance. Our collaborative efforts garnered multiple awards during that first year, culminating in a 3rd-place state trophy in the junior women's debate category.

Mrs. Ellis, eager to decipher the secret to our success, apparently believed it involved dismantling dynamic duos. Consequently, our partnership dissolved as sophomores. My former partner teamed up with a new debate colleague, securing a state debate championship and the opportunity to compete nationally. I found myself with a fortuitous debate colleague, and while we may not have lit up the award stage, we forged a bond that has endured a lifetime.

Meanwhile, my flair for wearing comedy and tragedy masks found expression in various speech events, spanning from prose and poetry to dramatic interpretation, oratorical declamation, and humorous interpretation. This theatrical journey led me down countless paths, culminating in a memorable national competition where I clinched a 2nd place finish. My rendition of *"Having a Baby Can Be a Scream!"* would have had Joan Rivers rolling in the aisles!

Footnote: Before Mrs. Ellis passed away, a movie about her life was crafted titled *"The Whole Wide World."* Renee Zellweger portrayed Mrs. Ellis, and my sophomore debate partner, Michael Scott Myers, swapped the podium for a pen and became a screenwriting sensation, bagging the Best First Screenplay Award at the 1997 Independent Spirit Awards. Since I knew him from those humble debating days, catching up with this Hollywood royalty doesn't require a backstage pass!

Shoutout to an Unsung Hero: Mrs. Ellis was nothing short of extraordinary. To be candid, she was in such demand during those high school years that I often leaned on her right-hand accomplice and chief morale booster, Jude Bourque. He holds legendary status as my closest male friend in high school and the undercover cheerleader behind the scenes of my life when a male perspective has been needed.

On those rare occasions when Mrs. Ellis couldn't be reached, Jude seamlessly stepped in, offering nuggets of wisdom and invaluable life lessons to carry me forward on my journey to success. He remains the unwavering ray of sunshine that brightens every one of my days. I struggle to recall when he didn't drop everything to lend a sympathetic ear and gently nudge me away from life's precarious edges!

So, if you're afraid of public speaking, fear not! Start small, practice regularly, and focus on becoming a better listener and collaborator.

Remember, it's not just about delivering a killer speech; it's about connecting with others and fostering solid relationships. And who knows, maybe one day they'll make a movie about your life, too – with a hint of drama, a splash of humor, and a touch of charm.

5

Face Front

'Weaving early dreams into a career that's right in front of you'

WHAT DO YOU WANT TO BE WHEN YOU GROW UP?

The age-old question: *"What do you want to be when you grow up?"* Well, I can proudly say that my childhood dream of being Gretl from *"The Sound of Music"* set me on a career path that involved less singing and more résumé writing. The hills weren't exactly alive with the sound of my dream job.

As a credentialed résumé writer and career coach, I've mastered the *"fake it until you make it"* philosophy. Let's face it: every life is a résumé – full of unexpected twists and turns. So, if anyone dares to raise an eyebrow at your career journey, hit them with the classic IT line: *"Oh, that? It's not a bug; it's a feature – my career's just playing hard to get,"* keeping inquiring minds on their toes like a classically trained ballet dancer!

Acting/Singing/Dancing Career Achieved: Behold my triumphs in the elusive realms of acting, singing, and dancing – a trifecta that defies convention and embraces the quirks of my eclectic journey. Witness my meteoric rise from the illustrious title of Wrap Accountant in a Cannon Films production *(though, regrettably, uncredited)* to the avant-garde portrayal of Roberta, the Killer in a tantalizing indie film that was never released *(maybe it had to escape).*

A thespian of versatile talents, I also landed a national TV slot as a stand-in for the lead character in the inaugural year of the Oprah Winfrey Network's *"Mystery Diagnosis"* premiere.

Little did I know, my childhood desire of becoming Gretl would weave a narrative more mesmerizing than the most intricate script. Who cares about credited roles when you've dabbled into the mystique of Wrap Accounting, portrayed a killer with unmatched panache, and tackled medical mysteries on a national stage? Apparently, yearning to be Gretl was the serendipitous passcode to unlocking a riotous array of cinematic quests.

Fortunately, I've mastered the art of not taking any of these showbiz shenanigans too seriously!

WHAT SKILLS CAN BE HONED FOR YOUR CAREER?

In the hallowed halls of high school, my dream of becoming a cheerleader took an unexpected turn, veering left into the surprising world of leading the high school band as a majorette. Twirling prowess may not have been my forte, but my dazzling smile compensated for lacking aerial acrobatics. Despite the snickers and raised eyebrows, I pressed on, discovering the remarkable art of finding joy in every endeavor. Who knew that a dearth of twirling talent could be the express lane to a career in spreading happiness?

Amidst the grand high school symphony, our modest 40-member band may have played the underdog's anthem, but this audacious soul was set on waltzing through the musical trenches. Behold, the majorette maestro, strutting with unapologetic flair, choreographing routines that screamed individuality louder than any brass instrument. And let's not overlook my unsung hero – Mom, the creative and visionary costume designer who stitched together my dreams trimmed with velvet and marabou. Through the dissonance of skepticism, I found my groove, for in the coolness hierarchy, nothing quite harmonizes like proudly parading in a marabou-draped majorette ensemble!

In the sweltering summer before my senior year, I was the lone majorette sent off to a twirling leadership camp. Let me be clear: this camp was tailor-made for majorette lines, usually accompanying larger bands and schools.

So, picture this: each time I stepped up to represent my school in the practice sessions, subtle snickers from the other competitors became my rite of passage.

At the camp's conclusion, awards were handed out, each more extravagant than the last - Best Head Majorette, Best Majorette Line, Best Use of Batons, and so forth, turning the whole affair into a baton-filled Oscars ceremony. Among the sea of 80 participants *(and yes, I counted),* I never imagined winning the prestigious title of Most Spirited Majorette.

A golden award for this unexpected honor dangles from my charm bracelet, a cheeky reminder that, sometimes, fiery enthusiasm outshines even the most perfect twirl.

Sage Advice: In 6th grade, I tried out for the middle school cheerleading squad. After almost an entire season of being relegated to sitting on the sidelines, recognizing my lack of talent, the cheer captain kept me on the bench, which was demoralizing. So, I quit. That night, I remember a phone call from a family friend, Bud Chalmers, when he sternly said, *"You're a quitter. I'm very disappointed in you. I want you to promise me you'll never quit again."* I took that promise to heart, and I never quit again.

Cheerleader-Adjacent Role: I may not have been the cheerleader I once aspired to be, but I found success in a cheerleader-adjacent role – leading others to success with positivity. Who needs pom-poms when you have a positive attitude?

So, the next time life throws an obstacle your way, remember you're not alone. We all have speed bumps, but how we approach them makes all the difference. After all, the hills might not be alive with the sound of music, but they are buzzing with the rhythm of life's unexpected adventures.

6

Facial Hair

'Motivating others through a generous heart'

Mom has always been drawn to troubled teenagers. She volunteered for years at our local halfway house for teenage boys who had lost their way. But little did we know, her journey would take a surprising turn during a movie outing to see *"A Star Is Born"* with Kris Kristofferson and Barbra Streisand.

Before its release, Kris got a sneak peek of the movie, witnessing his life unfold on the big screen. He was startled by scenes he couldn't remember filming, thanks to the alcohol-induced haze during filming. Talk about a *"plot twist"* in his own life! This revelation hit him like a ton of bricks, igniting a journey toward sobriety, which made this even more delicious for the media. Who would have guessed that watching the finished version for the first time would catapult Kris to bid the bottle farewell? Not even the scriptwriters saw that one coming.

As we witnessed this captivating story unfold, Mom found herself inspired to explore more of this songwriter's extensive catalog. Undoubtedly one of the greatest songwriters ever, selecting just one song proved to be a challenging task.

After much contemplation, she settled on the powerful track, *"Why Me, Lord."* Recognizing that the lyrics of its second verse, penned by a man who had navigated the repercussions of poor choices, would deeply resonate with the teenage residents of LJYA *(Lafayette Juvenile and Young Adult Program).*

"Try me, Lord, if you think there's a way
I can try to repay all I've taken from you.
Maybe, Lord, I can show someone else
what I've been through myself on my way back to you."

In her ceaseless effort to make a positive impact, Mom shared the remarkable tale of this now superstar's journey toward sobriety and redemption with the struggling teenagers. The story struck a chord with each resident, potentially transforming it into the ultimate inspirational anthem for rebellious teenagers.

Entertainment reports swarmed over this revelation. *"A Star Is Born"* wasn't just a showcase of Kris' acting chops; it unfolded into a blockbuster, highlighting his singing, songwriting, and hidden acting talents. His performance earned a Golden Globe Award for Best Actor, solidifying him as the real superstar in this unexpected story. Mom took things up a notch, as she was determined for Kris to understand the profound impact he was making on those troubled teens. Trying to get a letter to him turned into a red tape nightmare. And having him respond? Well, that was akin to discovering a pot of gold at the end of a rainbow – nothing short of extraordinary.

Neil Diamond, Elvis Presley, and even Marlon Brando were initially considered for the lead in "*A Star Is Born.*" If any of them had landed the role, Kris might never have had the chance to turn his life around. We would have missed this epic tale of redemption, and LJYA might not have received the financial boost from Kris's inspiring journey.

Through extensive research and unwavering persistence, Mom eventually got a note to Kris, informing him of the unbelievable impact his life had on the LJYA residents. Kris, with his heart of gold, even used his acts of random kindness to help fund LJYA. His story became a beacon of hope, proving that anyone can overcome challenges with motivation, perseverance, a little support – and a pinch of Hollywood magic.

Journal about your everyday experiences! Kris Kristofferson's story, shared with some persuasive writing and acts of kindness, became a blockbuster of inspiration to countless people. It reminds us that personal narratives can hit the emotional jackpot, connecting with the hearts of individuals and communities. Embrace the art of writing because your stories have the power to unfold and touch the hearts of those around you.

7

Setting and Facing Goals

'Achieving monumental goals without even realizing it'

Growing up with the caliber of athletes parading through our home was challenging enough. Another challenge was living in the formidable shadow of my overachieving older brother. He was my DNA success superhero, effortlessly succeeding academically without cracking a book, winning a high school student council election while on crutches, and collecting extracurricular accolades like baseball trading cards.

To this 8th-grader, that senior awards night felt like my big brother had won the triple crown... Class Valedictorian, numerous academic subject awards, and various other scholarships. It was a spectacular night for him. A build-up to the last award of the evening finally came.

The Torch Award was handed out each year to one male and one female graduating senior for standout achievement. That was the fateful evening when Louis Houston, a Renaissance man in our midst, clinched the male Torch Award. Louis had already been celebrated for his incredible brushstrokes, immortalizing our school mascot on the gymnasium wall. *(Years later, he earned a Ph.D. in Physics.)* With a list of life achievements rivaling the Magna Carta, the emcee wisely spared us the marathon recital, saving us from a night that might stretch into dawn.

Inspired by Louis' towering achievements, I began my journey for glory over the next four years. Determined to grasp the coveted Torch Award, I cast my net wide, enlisting in every club that would have me. I juggled academics and extracurriculars with the nimbleness of a trapeze artist, all in relentless pursuit of that shining prize.

Fast forward to my senior graduation, the climax of this plot. As the achievements of the female Torch Award recipient were announced, I underwent a momentary identity crisis until my involvement in speech and debate, band, and majorette activities lit up the room with a neon sign that screamed, *"Hey, it's Laurie Jankower!"* The relief and humility that accompanied receiving that 3-foot-tall trophy were so intense that I half expected a choir of angels to kick in.

Here's the kicker - my parents were utterly oblivious to my secret mission to earn the Torch Award. In their defense, I had not let them in on my private ambition. The best defense is a great offense, so Dad fired the multi-million-dollar question, *"Why didn't you tell us you were receiving this award? I didn't have my camera ready for a picture!"*

Lesson learned: blindsiding your parents with a colossal trophy at an important event is not the pinnacle of effective communication strategies.

So, as you ponder your dreams and aspirations, ask yourself: Are your goals realistic and purposeful, or are you reaching for the stars without a ladder? Do they align with your values, or are you chasing a trophy just because it's shiny? And most importantly, are you sharing them with your cheerleading section? Because, let's face it, every successful journey needs a squad cheering you on so they're not caught off guard at the award ceremony.

8

Funny Face

'Embracing humor can build self-confidence'

LET THE PARENTAL BATTLE BEGIN

Following in my brother's footsteps, I was ready to conquer the academic world at USL. Little did I know that college would be a battlefield of conflicting advice from my parents. Dad, the wise sage, dropped the academic bomb: *"Get a degree!"* Simple, straightforward, classic Dad advice. Then came Mom, with her unique perspective: *"Get a husband! Think of it as your MRS degree!"* Balancing these two pearls of wisdom felt like juggling bowling pins – a problematic act that could leave my love life and GPA scattered on the floor.

SUZIE HOMEMAKER OR NOT?

Enter the realm of career confusion. I decided to major in Fashion Merchandising, thinking it was a logical choice given my family's retail background. But, oh boy, did reality hit hard! The Home Economics department had other plans to mold me into a domestic goddess. Picture me, the culinary disaster, struggling in the Textiles Lab, pondering the flammability of polyester. Spoiler alert: I switched to the College of Business faster than you can say *"burnt polyester."*

After switching majors, I found the classes more aligned with my skills. My advantage was that our strict high school curriculum built a solid foundation that allowed me to soar.

Dad, ever the financial guru, reminded me that he'd only pay for four years of college *(what a vote of confidence)!* And, of course, the GPA had to stay above 3.0 to get that elusive car insurance discount. I often hovered just below that magical number, making car insurance lectures a recurring theme in college life. It's hilarious now, but not so much back then.

Mom's marital nudge was trickier than Dad's request. To fulfill her focus, I attended every social event possible. This balance of social life and academics affected my grades, as you can imagine. Growing up in a highly sheltered environment, I was a *"good girl." (That label is the kiss of death in college!)* Guys were happy to ask me for an initial date, but they never seemed to follow up with a second date invitation. I had a social calendar filled with first dates! This reality drove my self-esteem downward. I embraced the *"Freshman 15"* a term used for co-eds who gain extra weight during that first year of college because of the freedom that a college atmosphere allows and the bad habits picked up by fellow students.

Then came the infamous campus fraternity Scavenger Hunt. Imagine frat guys approaching me, not for a date, but searching for *"Laurie Jankower's lipstick."* My neon orange lipstick became the talk of campus, and I learned a valuable lesson – always make your own lipstick choices.

Years later, I turned that lipstick disaster into a successful career as a Mary Kay Independent Beauty Consultant. Talk about a full-circle moment! I also joined the Air Force ROTC to meet clean-cut boys and like-minded souls, not for a military career. Little did I know, I'd be recruited into Angel Flight, become a "Little Major" *(yes, it's real),* and even earn the Military Ball Queen crown. Suddenly, my dating prospects expanded exponentially. Thank you, ROTC!

Don't let me forget the unforgettable Human Sexuality course. In a class of 25, the written questionnaire handed out on the first day revealed that 96% were not virgins. The class collectively pointed at me, the lone virgin, as if Captain Obvious had joined our ranks that day. Lesson learned: Never underestimate the power of statistical irony.

Impactful Course: Dr. Nelda Spinks taught a standout required course in Technical Writing with love and dedication. Little did I know that her emphasis on résumé writing would significantly define and catapult my career.

Lesson Learned: When all was said and done, dad's sage advice led to a 3.0 GPA and a Bachelor of Science in Business Administration in precisely four years. Mom might have had different hopes, but success comes in many forms, and the path is never a straight line.

Worth Mentioning: After my maternal grandmother passed away, Mom and I embarked on the melancholy task of clearing out her apartment. As we cautiously approached her pristine kitchen, a moment of hesitation preceded our decision to crack open the oven door. With a wry chuckle, Mom quipped, "We probably ought to take a peek." To our amazement, hidden behind that oven door lay a decade's worth of tax returns – no kidding! The familial trait of domestic disarray resonates deeply in our family genes!

Laughter is the best medicine. Embrace the humor in life, find joy in the little things, and never underestimate the power of neon orange lipstick to turn a disaster into a triumph. After all, we're all funny occasionally, and a good laugh keeps us grounded in this crazy journey called life. So, let the parental battle continue, and may the comedic twists in your educational pursuit bring laughter to your soul.

9

Staring Life in the Face

'Exploring all career options is part of the process'

After graduating from USL in 1983, I sprinted into the world of work, armed with a degree and a graduation gift that shouted, *"Let's do this!"* – a buying trip to NYC. Because, you know, nothing says adulting like navigating the fashion scene in the Big Apple.

Reality hit when I realized New York buying trips weren't full-time gigs. Cue the universal post-grad question, *"Oh heck, I just graduated! Now what?"*

Considering a television career seemed like an exciting idea after the NYC glitz. Following my heart, I applied to the local CBS affiliate, thinking, *"Why not?"* Meanwhile, I had another tempting offer: radio sales near Comptche, California. Picture me contemplating a life selling radio ads in a place with a rural population of 120 people *(that's a one and a two).* My parents wisely nudged me out of this fiasco, saving me from a potentially solitary life with radio waves.

My next stop was San Antonio, with grand plans to earn an MBA at the University of Texas at Austin. Spoiler alert: the campus was enormous, but my plans were not, and I quickly reconsidered. During my job-hunting despair, a cousin with an executive position at USAA swooped in with an offer. Working 10 hours a day, four days a week? Intriguing. Sound company? Absolutely. Insurance? Not exactly my fashion-forward dream, but a job is a job.

Just as I was gearing up for the USAA interview, the CBS affiliate back home rang, offering an interview for the news department. Cue the dramatic turnaround, packed bags, and a swift return to Lafayette. The News Director, Maria Placer, grilled me for two hours. Intimidated yet fascinated, I somehow landed the role of Office Manager / News Secretary role for KLFY TV 10.

Life in the news department was a whirlwind – copy changes, hair-pulling directors, and a relentless race against the clock. I played the role of the unsung hero, keeping the news team sane. Answering phones, delivering messages, and typing up news copy – in my mind, I was the glue holding this chaotic newsroom together. My goal? To be the *"little sister"* mascot of the news department, behind the scenes and loving it. To boost my morale, I remembered birthdays and even attempted baking.

One late-night cookie adventure turned into a missed deadline, but perfection was never my goal. My dream of a career in TV took a toll – my waist-length hair was falling out, and the stress was palpable. A one-year contract turned into my eat-sleep-breathe-TV reality. I resigned, knowing that this wasn't my forever path, but it opened doors to a multitude of new opportunities.

After the sands of time trickled away, I embraced the necessary art of pruning my career bonsai shrub. It turned out that my professional journey required a trim to reveal the exquisite tree within. While the realm of TV wasn't my ultimate destination, the adventure felt like a carnival ride, complete with valuable lessons, moments of uproarious laughter, and, yes, a few missed cookie deadlines. Because, let's face it, life's journey is best savored with a side of humor.

Deep within each of us lies a beautiful and delicate bonsai tree, patiently waiting for its moment of revelation from the inside out. The pruning process, though challenging, is the essential step required for future growth and flourishment.

10

Facing Challenges

'Transitioning life's obstacles into a productive career, one job at a time'

Ah, the delightful journey from "Just Over Broke" *(aka JOBS)* to finding a career. My story is a loop-de-loop of job mishaps, fired on day one, fired on day two, and culinary experiences with cheesecake. Brace yourself for the sidesplitting job-hopping saga:

Gift Wrapper: The tale began with my dazzling debut as a gift-wrapper extraordinaire in our family's retail business. I was part of the 5th generation that would work hard to learn about our legacy. Spoiler alert: I was handed my walking papers on day one! Yes, the family business bid farewell because my wrapping skills fell short of present-worthy standards.

Bookkeeper: My next audition, the enthralling world of debits and credits. Who knew accounting could be so confusing? Spoiler alert: Fired on day two because crunching numbers just didn't compute for me. Obviously, I wasn't balanced enough for the ledger!

Advertising Assistant: On day three, Dad, my knight in shining armor, rescued me with a crucial question - *"Can you type?"* Bingo! Office line, here I come. No more wrapping disasters or accounting headaches. This was the start of something beautiful. This lasted through the rest of that Christmas holiday break, and then school beckoned.

Fashion Buyer: After earning a high school diploma, I set sail for a weeklong adventure in NYC – one of the world's fashion capitals. Picture this: Dining in delicatessens that served cheesecake the size of a small planet, Broadway musicals, and my first solo buying assignment. My mission was to purchase 125 units with a $5,000 budget in one day. I aced it, buying 124 units for $5,210. Mission accomplished! Take that, NYC!

Hand Stamper: College brought fresh challenges, like being the hand-stamping maestro at a local bar. Two-hour shifts, $35 – a college student's dream job. Easy and low-skill – the perfect combo.

Advertising Assistant (encore): Internship o'clock and Dillard's welcomed me in. Proofing ads, typing documents, and directing – déjà vu with the same cast from my family business days. It was a different stage and the same chaos, but this time, there was no firing squad; I aced the internship instead!

Retail Assistant Manager: A revelation! Sometimes, you need a job you despise to discover your true calling. Micromanaging supervisor? Check. Contractual escape from the staffing agency? Double-check. Resigning within three months? Absolutely.

Bank Teller: A big move to a nearby city led me to a new challenge – the teller position at a credit union seemed like the perfect fit. My senior colleagues didn't quite see eye-to-eye with me... literally. With my vertical challenge, counting and wrapping coins became my circus act – a short gal, a tall counter, and a line of customers waiting for the show. Clearly, change was needed – pun intended!

And there you have it, my illustrious journey from job to job, learning, laughing, and occasionally being handed a pink slip. Who knew cheesecake and counting coins could be such pivotal moments? Life's a sitcom, and I'm trying to find the right channel!

11

Putting On A Brave Face

'Moving out of your comfort zone'

Behold, this daring soul armed with $8,000 in savings, orchestrating a covert migration from Louisiana to the wild frontiers of Los Angeles. Leaving behind an apartment bursting with belongings was a splendid surprise for my unsuspecting parents. Dreams? Oh, dreams galore!

The first stop was a Club Med resort in Mexico, unbeknownst to me, a hotbed for mingling singles. Nude body painting was on the agenda, and alcohol flowed like candy on Halloween. Too bad I'm not a drinker – wasted opportunities everywhere! Imagine Gidget on a wild vacation, desperately trying to fit into the cocktail-fuel chaos.

Fast forward to the golden state of California, where the challenge awaited – breaking the news to my parents. Dad had a meltdown, but Mom, the eternal optimist, assured him it would all work out. This chick needed to fly the coop, leaving behind an apartment full of stuff for my family to deal with. Self-absorbed? Definitely! But the bandage had to be ripped off so I could go after those sunny California dreams.

With a $400 clothing budget, it was time for a wardrobe upgrade. The GAP was my savior, and their "sale" items made expensive California somewhat affordable. Haircut time! I found a Vidal Sassoon Academy offering free haircuts – catch? I had to let the stylist unleash her creativity. Results? Gorgeous in the front, McDonald's Golden Arches shaved into the back of my head. I pretended to love it, but reality hit as I returned to my hotel. Emergency solution? A Wheaties box featuring Mary Lou Retton's face and a budget-friendly barber miraculously transformed me into her doppelganger. Who says dreams can't be *'cereal killers?'*

Venturing into the unknown with faith demands a cocktail of courage, adaptability, thoughtfulness for others, resourcefulness, and a delightful sense of humor to navigate the unpredictable journey. As Thomas Edison wisely said, "I have not failed. I've just found 10,000 ways that won't work." Cheers to the unconventional, and may the journey be as bold as the dreams!

12

Self-Effacing

'Gaining confidence and inspiration from a behind-the-scenes career mentor'

Oh, the cosmic comedy of life in Los Angeles – where angels *(and maybe some aspiring screenwriters)* fear to tread! Let's unfold this serendipitous tale...

Picture it: A Louisiana transplant armed with dreams and a résumé in dire need of Hollywood sparkle. Little did I know, my guardian angel was lurking in a Santa Monica copy shop, probably next to the coffee machine that dispenses divine intervention.

In April '85, I stumbled into this print shop, praying for résumé magic. The owner, probably a retired genie, handed me the winning ticket – a business card for Pam Mammet, résumé writer extraordinaire.

This wasn't just a referral but God's intervention, complete with voicemail technology. Pam, the quiet introvert who probably had more friends in her typewriter than in real life, became my savior. Imagine me, a bundle of nerves, leaving voicemail messages as if auditioning for a movie role. And guess what? She called back! An in-person meeting was arranged – cue the celestial trumpets!

Despite her shy nature, Pam embraced me like a long-lost cousin. And get this: She agreed to craft my résumé on an old-school typewriter. That completed document was smoother than the silk lining of the most exquisite wedding gown ever. The cost? Let's just say it was a bargain paid in laughter and friendship coupons.

Armed with Pam's résumé masterpiece, I hit several major studios as if auditioning for the lead in their next blockbuster hit. Paramount Pictures? Check. Lorimar? Check. Confidence level? Through the Hollywood sign! Result: I landed a gig at Panavision. My Hollywood dream was alive, and Pam was my backstage pass.

Now Pam, despite her self-effacing nature and agoraphobia, had become my apartment fairy godmother. She arranged for a friend to rent me space for $100 a month. Move-in day was a nightmare turned into a comedy show – but we survived. Pam, who braved West Hollywood for me, deserved an honorary Oscar for *"Best Supporting Friend in a Résumé Drama."*

But it wasn't just about jobs and résumés; Pam gave me more therapy than a Hollywood shrink. *"Pam Therapy"* was the best, minus the leather couch and hourly rates. Her friendship and kind heart saved me from a Hollywood-sized therapy bill.

Fast forward to Pam's heroic battle with cancer. She fought like a superhero, probably armed with a résumé of her accomplishments. Our friendship outlived my time in California by 18 years – just like the hit TV series M*A*S*H which lasted longer than the Korean War it portrayed.

Pam was a legendary friend who kept sending care packages, even after I hightailed it back to Louisiana. The postal service probably thought she was a part-time angel.

Pivot: Here's to Pam – my champion in the City of Angels. If not for her that first week in LA, my life could have been more dramatic than a daytime soap opera.

Lesson learned: When in Los Angeles, seek résumé help, but also watch out for unexpected mentors who type their way into your heart. Amen, Pam!

When vulnerability and great need intersect, the right person will always appear if you ask. This person might be an unlikely source of blessings if you invite God to walk with you on the journey.

WELCOME TO HOLLYWOOD. WHAT'S YOUR DREAM?

Los Angeles in the '80s was a whirlwind of excitement. There I was, a Louisiana soul swept up in the frenzy of Hollywood dreams.

After months of navigating the labyrinth of LA without finding gainful employment *(no surprise there),* I played the parental card and reached out to Jamie Barber, a friend my folks had met on a cruise years ago. After revealing my lineage, I landed a job on the spot! My debut role? Expendables Receptionist – the departmental gatekeeper who scheduled appointments and fielded calls. Living the Hollywood dream, minus the red carpet, but with a hefty side of culture shock.

Working at Cinepro, the Hollywood arm of Panavision, taught me one thing – the movie industry moves at its own pace. I got to rub elbows with Elliott Gould, Kareem Abdul Jabar, and Esther Williams. And though Madonna was in the building, we mere mortals weren't VIP enough to meet her.

However, the glamorous façade of LA often concealed its gritty underbelly, a reality I encountered firsthand. Tagging along with a friend to a gathering, I was greeted at the door with an offer for some *"coke."* My response? *"Sure, I'll have a Diet Coke!"* (I noticed laughter from other guests and realized our definitions of "coke" were drastically different!)

Battling the haze of an outdoor Bruce Springsteen concert, I found myself inhaling more than just the music, catching a second-hand contact high from the marijuana being smoked all around me. Yet, as the concert faded into memory, the allure of a hot fudge sundae proved to be the perfect antidote to my unexpected *"munchies."* Welcome to the Wild Side, Louisiana girl!

One memorable escapade led me to a *Rustler's Rhapsody* screening party, where I came face-to-face with an actual Academy Award. It was proudly showcased in a glass case for all to admire. Talk about a monumental thrill!

Then came July 1985 – the *Back to the Future* premiere. When *'Steven Spielberg presents'* showed up on the movie screen, everyone cheered with excitement. I was fortunate to sit next to one of the movie extras, and we all felt the electricity in the air.

But beyond the glitz, LA was grappling with the AIDS epidemic and intense road rage on the world-famous Ventura Freeway. Bumper stickers screamed, *"Cover me, I'm changing lanes"* – a snapshot of the LA madness.

In another twist, I secured a spot-on *Love Connection,* the iconic '80s reality dating show! Though I clinched the date, the post-date discussion on live TV unequivocally marked it as the worst date of my life. Classic Chuck Woolery confirmed it in the elevator afterward, *"That guy was a jerk!"*

After a few months of LA adventures, the homesickness hit me like a ton of bricks. Luckily, Jamie, the gem of a boss, understood. The crew threw me a going-away bash and gifted me an official movie-industry mirrored clapboard. It's proudly displayed in my office, a glitzy reminder of my LA escapades.

So, there you have it - my tale of LA dreams, unexpected opportunities, and a Love Connection disaster. Life is a movie, and I was a Louisiana belle trying to find her scene in the Hollywood script. Who knew Club Med in Mexico could be the opening scene to a blockbuster life-changing story?

13

Facing Trial

'Putting an entrepreneurial future to the test in a tumultuous economic crisis'

The '80s were also the era of big hair, questionable fashion choices, and, for me - a dizzying spin from the oil crisis to mastering countless trades!

In early 1986, Louisiana felt the impact - the unfortunate Space Shuttle Challenger disaster and the oil bust dealt a double blow. As the office manager for eight oil-and-gas-related companies, I can confirm that the challenge and economic turmoil were intense. Typewriters became my trusty allies, and my savings clocked in at a modest $200 – technically broke but not broken in spirit. I dubbed it the *'Oil Bust Tango,'* where every step was choreographed on 'typewriter' keys.

Our town, deeply dependent on the oil and gas industry, witnessed the Chamber of Commerce's "*I Believe in Lafayette*" campaign taking a local twist – '*I Be Leavin' Lafayette.*' Quite a turn of phrase, and not in a good way. As a résumé writer, I witnessed many fleeing to brighter opportunities elsewhere, prompting our community to diversity and redefine itself for stability and economic growth.

Kudos to Chris Pettus, the Petroleum Landman who set up my first business, Just Your Type, Inc. Tough times, indeed, but Chris, armed with his oil money magic wand, transformed my broken typewriter tale into a startup Cinderella story. Those Articles of Incorporation? My golden ticket to startup stardom.

But reality hit the region hard, and the oil and gas industry vanished like a Houdini act. I had to downsize – my office moved from business chic to apartment casual. Suddenly, my résumé business became my roommate, and I typed countless documents on the dining table. The first month barely brought in $350 through word of mouth, while the rent demanded a hefty $400. The struggle was so real that I even started selling belongings just to keep afloat. I would've considered subletting my coffee maker if I could've afforded one in the first place!

Then came the epiphany – the typewriter was hindering my hustle. A line typed, a mistake made, and poof, a fresh sheet of paper. A genius move was in order. So, I embraced technology – the computer became my knight in shining plastic, making me the Steve Jobs of résumé writing. I wasn't the most accurate typist but could hit 'delete' like a boss.

With a stealthily arranged $1,000 loan from Dad *(courtesy of Mom's covert operations),* I boldly plunged into the digital realm. Armed with my newfound funds, I splurged on a shiny new computer and state-of-the-art laser printer, bidding a fond farewell to my faithful typewriter of yore. Despite Dad's skepticism regarding my tech skills, I swiftly proved him wrong – evolving into the Indiana Jones of résumé solutions!

I danced the delicate act of a substitute teacher to keep the lights on in those early months because, let's face it, being a startup wizard doesn't always conjure up immediate riches. Nonetheless, armed with determination, an entrepreneurial spirit, and faith as vast as the ocean, I made a solemn vow to steer the choppy waters of my venture toward the shores of success.

From there, my résumé writing business blossomed. I grew into a successful résumé writer and career coach, happily cheering on clients to succeed with the enthusiasm of a hyperactive mascot on a caffeine bender.

Diving headfirst into the world of industry credentials, I made it my mission to blaze trails and be Louisiana's trendsetting pioneer. *(I quickly learned that being the first to do something comes with the perk of no pressure to be the best – after all, no one's ever done it before!)* That mindset has always fueled my drive to be the first, not necessarily the best! Reflecting on those 18 years, I steered over 12,000 clients toward their career dreams.

As my business evolved, JYT Media emerged as the launching pad for expansion, further igniting my passion to grow our team and venture into the thrilling realms of graphic design and website development.

Soon after the internet emerged, I answered with HitTheMall.com. During that year, achieving success through e-commerce felt as daunting as keeping a kayak afloat during a hurricane – thrilling yet incredibly challenging.

Although HitTheMall.com took a swan dive, I emerged with pride in my earnest attempt. What doesn't kill you makes you stronger – and it certainly taught me to avoid online mall ventures without adequate capital.

Career Validation: Looking back on the pivotal decision to purchase my first new car in '92, Dad stepped into the spotlight, offering unwavering support and confidence in my knack for savvy decisions rooted in intuition and experience. As he uttered those magic words, *"You can afford it,"* it dawned on me: it wasn't just about the car; it spoke volumes. Firstly, Dad beamed with genuine pride at my achievements. Secondly, he acknowledged that my finesse in negotiations, refined through coaching clients in their salary battles, was bearing fruit in real-world situations.

Blind faith, a positive attitude, and a great sense of humor can turn an obsolete typewriter into a résumé writing career. Sometimes, all it takes is a typo and a dream!

14

Facial Recognition

'Seeing through the eyes of an honest public servant'

You may think you've heard all about the wild world of Louisiana politics, but have you ever considered that a sophisticated laser printer could be your entrance ticket?

There I was, fully engrossed in growing my new venture, Just Your Type, Inc., typing away at my keyboard when Ron Gomez called out of the blue. Ron, a brilliant man of the people had effortlessly secured re-election without any opposition – a Louisiana State Representative with a VIP connection list rivaling U.S. President Ronald Reagan at the time. Ron needed a reliable, honest, and resourceful employee. Plus, he had a soft spot for my computer and laser printer, as Ron was attempting to embrace technology himself!

Surprisingly, I landed the job without an interview. Wondering why? As it turns out, Ron had a connection with my family through USL sports, and our paths had crossed back in first grade when his son and I were classmates. Was it fate or merely a shared fascination with laser printers? I'll never know.

Being the astute man of the people, Ron proposed that I run my business through his office. Why not? My laser printer could infuse a bit of glamour into his official correspondence, giving it the look and feel of the Declaration of Independence – but with an extra touch of laser-printed flair.

Teaming up with Ron felt like a divine pairing straight out of Louisiana lore. After Dad, Ron easily clinched the title of best male boss I ever had. Period. While he tackled legislative matters, I confidently and efficiently managed his Lafayette office. The role included the added perks of a second income with benefits – all thanks to my trusty printer, playing a crucial supporting role in this adventure.

As Ron's aide, I became the gatekeeper of his Lafayette office – answering calls, screening constituents, and handling occasional calls about sports because Ron was the *"Voice of the Cajuns."* If a constituent was upset, it was typically because their social security checks were fashionably late. Cue the federal issue referral to then U.S. Congressman Jimmy Hayes.

But the real kicker? Ron's grand reveal in 1990. The good news? He earned a promotion to the Governor's Executive Cabinet. The bad news? I was out of a job. Classic Ron! He had more finesse in delivering the news than I had ever seen. And the punchline? *"Well, it did take a staff of 300 to replace you!"* Bravo, Ron, bravo!

In the grand dance of Louisiana politics, I learned that sometimes you're just a pawn in the game. It was a two-year ride – a crash course in handling life's challenges with a smile. Thanks, Ron, for the printer narrative and the unforgettable stint in public service.

Life might throw an occasional knuckleball, but you can turn those slow pitches into grand slams with a good sense of humor. Buckle up, enjoy the ride, and remember, sometimes it's not about the printer – it's about the people you meet along the way!

15

Facing The Music

'Living without music is unimaginable'

In the symphony of my musically gifted family, I found myself knee-deep in the grand melodies. Florence Adler, my great-grandmother (aka Nana), earned K.H. Shepard's *"Best Pianist"* accolades *(circa 1904, 1905)*. My paternal grandfather, Edel, the maestro of the silent movie era, painted scenes with live piano tunes in movie theatres. Dad added his jazzy flair to the saxophone, while Mom effortlessly played piano by ear and serenaded with a voice that could charm the birds. Aunt Barbara dreamt of a violin virtuoso career, and then there's me – the vocal performer wannabe. If life were a Broadway musical, our family might be portrayed as a harmonious blend of notes and nostalgia with a touch of theatrical whimsy.

A GRAND NIGHT FOR SINGING

2003 held special significance for our community as we joined the rest of Louisiana in commemorating the Louisiana Purchase Bicentennial. As part of the festivities, the Abbey Players *(a local community theatre group)* hosted a fundraising event featuring the Rodgers and Hammerstein musical *"A Grand Night for Singing."* The Louisiana Purchase marked a pivotal moment in our nation's history, and this theatrical contribution would help our community participate in the statewide celebration.

However, I found myself facing personal challenges. Returning to live with my parents, I grappled with the heart-wrenching decline of my father's health due to his Parkinson's disease diagnosis. This unexpected turn shook our family to its core, and I felt compelled to be by his side through every moment of his struggle.

In this period of upheaval, with my social life virtually nonexistent, I settled into a nightly routine of snuggling in my gown and robe by 7pm and watching TV with the caregivers who lovingly tended to my father each night. During these solitary evenings, I stumbled upon shows like *"American Idol"* and *"The Bachelor,"* offering a brief distraction from the sad reality of my circumstances. In late April, a ray of hope pierced through the darkness in the form of an unexpected call from my friend, Shawn Roy. He reached out to enlist my help for a colleague in need. That conversation lasted about 30 minutes. As the call ended, I distinctly remember Shawn asking, *"I forgot to ask ... you CAN sing, right?"* I replied, *"Um, I can carry a tune!!"* Amazingly, my lack of confidence in that answer didn't dissuade Shawn from helping me land an audition!!

It turned out that the third female role in the upcoming Abbey Players musical had left the show just days before rehearsals began. Shawn, aware of my passion for performing, asked if I would consider auditioning. Despite my circumstances at home, I gratefully jumped at this chance.

Armed with every sheet of Rodgers and Hammerstein music in my collection, I strutted into the interview the following evening and met with the production's director – Wade Russo. *(Little did I realize at the time that Wade boasted a remarkable Broadway résumé, having worked with Julie Andrews and other heavy-hitting talents!)*

I belted out "I Can't Say No" from the musical *'Oklahoma,'* hitting every note with the biggest grin I could muster. It was the perfect piece to flaunt my singing prowess, especially since it allowed me to drop the bombshell that my community theatre debut was in that very musical. Oh, and did I mention that Mom, a die-hard fan of the show since its inception, named me after the lead character, Laurey? I thought with that tidbit, I'd be a shoo-in for the part.

While Wade was kind during my audition, he confessed that he sought a higher soprano voice than mine. I was disappointed. As I gathered my books to leave gracefully, I stalled by asking him who the other cast members were. When he mentioned the other names, I got VERY excited!

One had originated a role on Broadway. Lucky for the local production, he was in town handling some family business. Another was one of Mom's favorite students when she taught high school. The third was a vocalist I had hired while serving as music director at a local church. I also felt her sister *(another cast member)* possessed the vocals to carry a big show like this. The final cast member was a vocal student with whom I had collaborated during my years with the university choir. Everyone in the production brought a familiar comfort when I heard the roster.

Feeling like Wade wouldn't be casting me anyway, I decided to throw caution to the wind and share my two cents. *"If I were directing the show,"* I boldly declared, *"I'd switch the other soprano to the ingénue role and then slide myself in for comedy and heavy lifting behind the scenes."* My honesty may have caught him off guard, but I was determined to land a spot in that show no matter what! After a brief moment of collaboration with his assistant director, Wade returned with a curious expression.

He said, *"Here's the script! We need you here in two days to start rehearsals!"* I was on cloud nine!! I couldn't believe that he responded to my gumption!

The musical rehearsals were daunting, but I never missed a beat. My dedication to participating in this six-person review felt pivotal and invigorating to my very core. I understood that this experience would help me shift my focus and traverse through personal drama, preparing me for other life-changing moments.

When desperation meets opportunity, magic happens. Living with my parents and binge-watching American Idol and The Bachelor, I felt like my social life had taken an early retirement. But a phone call from a dear friend, changed the score.

An unexpected audition, a candid chat with the director, and there I was, part of a Broadway-seasoned cast. Never underestimate the power of a bold suggestion and a touch of musical magic.

A CAPELLA NATIONAL ANTHEM

Fast forward to my anthem adventures. Singing the national anthem became my way of honoring my late father, a U.S. Air Force veteran. From professional events to charity functions, I'd proudly belt out the anthem whenever asked.

A profoundly defining moment was the tragic backdrop of 9/11. Singing confidently at a business expo that week, I held it together until reality hit as I left the stage. The tears flowed, and in that moment, the true weight of the tragedy sank in. Since then, I've been honored to sing the national anthem at every event level, from Little League championships to Olympic trials that have streamed worldwide. What an honor!

Pivot: The national anthem isn't just a song; it's a tribute and a connection to our military loved ones. It's about channeling emotions, not just vocal skills. Singing with purpose, the anthem becomes a bridge between us and those who've served, a reminder of what it truly means to be patriotic.

Find your passion, and let it serenade your life. When opportunity knocks, answer confidently – even if it's a phone call asking if you can audition with questionable singing skills. Life's a Broadway show, and you're the star. Encore, anyone?

16

To Love Another Person is to See the Face of God

'Recognizing God's blatant signs'

My life can be summarized with this timeless line from Victor Hugo's Les Misérables, *"To love another person is to see the face of God."* My journey from the heart of Cajun country in Lafayette, LA, to the spotlight of faith is not for the faint of heart.

The life lessons of love Mom taught me directly resulted from her upbringing in San Antonio, Texas. Her grandparents ensured that theirs was an extremely close-knit group. The generation above Mom's was even closer, as the three male siblings were referred to as "the boys," and the two girls would check in on each other several times a day. Paw Paw *(Mom's father)* made frequent mission trips to visit a friend who was in constant contact with the leper colony in Carville, Louisiana. This was not a normal thing in those days. However, it's a true lesson of love shared through the years.

Growing up in south Louisiana as part of the Mervine Kahn family, known for starting and growing businesses while giving back to the community, I had a front-row seat to a legacy at the heart of Cajun country. Envision accordions, pianos, the best food on the planet, and the friendliest people you'll ever meet. The Catholic surroundings made Mom's love for festive décor and those Christmas decorations for my Jewish family permissible. But imagine little me, fresh out of 2nd grade, singing *"Jesus Loves Me This I Know, For the Bible Tells Me So."* Mom, bless her heart, tried to explain why that wasn't our jam, but my logic was rock-solid: Jesus was a Jewish man, just like us, out to save the world. Mom was speechless – my theological chapter had begun!

Then came the mid-semester switch in 7th grade to a Catholic school. Dress code woes *(Why did the girls have to wear uniforms of ugly brown pleated skirts and white blouses when the guys could wear whatever they wanted?),* unfamiliar prayers, and mandatory masses led my teenage brain spiraling into a hygiene crisis during those weekly, hour-long masses.

During the solemnity of the mass, my mind wandered – with the kneeling student behind me positioned at or near my scalp, I fretted over whether I had remembered to wash my hair that morning.

While I remained oblivious to the sermon, I couldn't ignore the significant changes my teenage body was undergoing. The struggle was real.

THE PIVOTAL CLASS THAT CHANGED MY LIFE

But hold your rosary, there's a twist! Brother Richard Arnandez, my Freshman Religion Teacher, was a powerhouse. Former Secretary General of Christian Brothers in Rome *(who reported directly to the Pope during that time),* made religion class a spiritual Broadway show.

He took me under his wing and even positioned me front and center in the class on day one. He leaned over and whispered in my ear, *"Take good notes in this class."* Then he called the first class to order and said, *"Welcome to Freshman Religion Class. This year, we will learn about the history of the Catholic Church and the Jewish People."* This caught my ear and ignited an eagerness to learn that I had never experienced before. Did this teacher know the answers I needed? Could this be a turning point in my life? Would I finally comprehend what everyone else in the class already knew? As instructed, I took amazing notes. When our first exam of the year came up, Brother Richard told us to bring our notebooks to class. After he handed out the tests, he said, *"Take out your notebooks because this is an open-notebook test!"* I had taken copious notes and scored the highest in the class! This trend lasted the entire year, and I earned the Freshman Religion Award. When that award was revealed, my poor parents had no idea how to react!

Sex Education was also part of that Freshman Religion curriculum. The guys were escorted into another room and trained by Br. Richard. The girls remained in the classroom and were taught by a female instructor. She used visuals and spoke a language that I just didn't comprehend. Br. Richard and the guys returned to class, and I was bewildered. Before moving on, that wonderful

Christian Brother asked the girls if anyone had questions. I sheepishly raised my hand and said, *"I don't understand."* Br. Richard smiled and said, *"If a boy takes you out on a date and then does something he shouldn't, just slap him across the face and tell him you're not that kind of girl! Understand?"* I did. There were chuckles throughout the room, but I got it.

Because of my response to Br. Richard, word got out, and my dating life was grim during those four years. It was not every high school guy's dream to ask me out. I participated in almost every "nerd" activity on campus: Math Club, Speech/Debate, Band, and National Honor Society. I was a good girl ... the kind a guy would marry but not the kind he would fool around with. I had to practically import guys to earn a place at school dances and other functions.

Open-book exams, winning the Freshman Religion Award, and a crash course in human sexuality as deemed curriculum-appropriate– it was a holy rollercoaster!

ANOTHER RELIGION TEACHER WHO MADE A LASTING IMPRESSION

Next up, Brother Phillip, a young, funny, and totally empathetic teacher toward my predicament. One of his class assignments was to create and display my story on the bulletin board. Mom helped me develop the idea of putting a Cross and a Star of David side-by-side with the caption, *"Today is the First Day of the Rest of Your Life!"* I figured that marrying the Cross and the Star of David was good. Little did I realize how impactful this one assignment would be. The display went up Friday afternoon and was vandalized by Monday morning. Antisemitic remarks were scribbled across the torn-down display.

In typical fashion, I was worried about my grade, not about what had been done to my project. The classmates who vandalized it got reprimanded, which could have potentially affected their graduation status.

I somehow survived high school and the unfortunate prejudices that existed at that time. After graduating, I enrolled at USL.

SORORITY RUSH

After some gentle persuasion, I embarked on rushing a sorority, and I was recruited hard by several of the campus clubs. Before starting the rush week, however, a friend from high school pulled me aside to confide that her sorority wouldn't be extending a bid to me because of my religion. She felt terrible about it but didn't want me to be disappointed. The same was true for other sororities who didn't extend invitations to join. Knowing this beforehand made it easier for me to accept and move on.

The sorority I landed in was Chi Omega. These were the most admirable women, and I could be myself among them.

I joined Chi Omega because of the beautiful hearts of the women in this incredible group. And when the Chi Omega Symphony was shared during rush week, it epitomized the type of woman I wanted to become:

"To live constantly above snobbery of word or deed; to place scholarship before social obligations and character before appearances; to be in the best sense, democratic rather than "exclusive," and lovable rather than "popular"; to work earnestly, to speak kindly, to act sincerely, and to choose thoughtfully that course which occasion and conscience demand; to be womanly always; to be discouraged never; in a word, to be loyal under any and all circumstances to my Fraternity and her highest teachings and to have her welfare ever at heart that she may be a symphony of high purpose and helpfulness in which there is no discordant note."

This 'symphony' was penned by Ethel Switzer Howard during her own rush week in 1904. What an impactful and enduring statement!

Before my initiation, the officers shared that Chi Omega's mission statement was Hellenic Culture and Christian Ideals! They prayed I wouldn't be offended, saying I was the most Christian person they knew. Incredible Christian Brothers trained me at a parochial high school! Offended? I think not!

GOD'S AMAZING SEEDS WERE BEING PLANTED

Several years after college, we laid to rest Mr. Robert Mahtook, one of our cherished family friends. He epitomized kindness and warmth, and I often desired to marry someone with his qualities. At his funeral, his eldest son, Robbie, was called upon *(at the last second)* to deliver the eulogy, as the family priest was too distraught to speak. Despite the circumstances, Robbie rose to the occasion with grace.

Meanwhile, Sarah Mahtook, the widow, sang during the service without missing a note, displaying remarkable faith. Following the funeral, I was thrust into an unexpected conversation – not with the somber souls offering condolences, but with Jesus, who made a divine appearance in the recesses of my heart.

Back at my apartment, post-funeral, I collapsed onto the living room carpet, engaging in a full-blown sob fest. It was then, in the midst of my emotional meltdown, that I had a heart-to-heart with heaven. I confessed that I needed Him in my life.

But being my ever-doubtful mortal self, I asked Him to wait until I turned 30 to see if I could figure life out solo. I would ask Him to take over if I couldn't do it without Him. Boy, was I ignorant to ask that!

Faithful to my word, I joined the church in my 30th year. And getting to live this unexpected news with Karen, my best friend, was icing on the cake! God had given us both a blatant sign of His divine presence!!

I asked Robbie Mahtook, who delivered that beautiful eulogy for his father, to serve as my godfather. During the commemoration, I received the holy trifecta - Baptism, First Communion, and Confirmation – an existential booster shot of epic proportions!

There was a humorous note in my grandmother's reaction to news of my conversion. Despite her initial sign of *"Darn, we lost another one,"* I discovered her secret stint in a Catholic school for 12 years. *(Way to bury the lead, Mama Bea!)* Her timely departure on Good Friday - coinciding with Jesus - felt like a divine nudge. After all, if you could choose heavenly ascension, Good Friday guarantees you top-tier company!

EMBRACING MUSIC AS A CHURCH CALLING

I have always loved music and was in several musicals and community theater productions throughout college. It wasn't until I turned Catholic, however, that my real music ministry came out.

I've served as a cantor and active member of several church choirs in the area. Singing for weddings and funerals is another experience I cherish as a great way to share my faith.

While going through a difficult time, I approached a priest at a new church, advising him that he needed a cantor at masses. I felt the congregation needed prayer leadership through music.

I confessed, *"I have to sing!"* He said, *"I'm not hiring!"* I said, *"That doesn't matter. I HAVE to sing!"* So, he introduced me the following week, *"This is Laurie, and she says she has to sing!"* The priest probably rolled his eyes during the introduction, but God put music in my heart. It's one of my biggest blessings - to share God's word through music!!

Throughout my life, I've harbored a clandestine dream for world peace. During a week of emotional "Come, Lord Jesus!" prayer sessions, I finally shared this heartfelt desire with my group. And then, like a bolt from heaven, the realization struck me: The word Catholic means universal! Could it be that I've been treading on the right path? Only divine intervention can unveil this answer!

I'm living proof that converts make the best Catholics. And I'm thriving in a weekly prayer group that continues to open my heart to God's will. Even the almighty has a punchline about conversion:

A Jewish son tells his father he is moving out. The son returns a year later and tells his father that he has converted to Christianity.

The father is upset and calls his friend, who is also Jewish. "You won't believe this. My son David moved out for a year and came back and told me he converted to Christianity."

His friend says, "You won't believe this... my son Benjamin moved away for a year, and when he came back, HE converted to Christianity too!"

Both upset, they call their rabbi and explain what happened. The rabbi says, "You won't believe this. My son Joshua moved away, and when HE came back, he told me he converted to Christianity too!"

The rabbi suggests they call God and tell Him. The rabbi tells God that all three men had sons who moved away and converted to Christianity and didn't know what to do. God says to them, "You won't believe this..."

A Passing Notion or Blatant Sign from God? My family hails from Rayne, Louisiana, affectionately known as the Frog Capital of the World due to its extensive frog exports nationwide. Interestingly, the acronym **FROG** stands for ***Fully Rely on God.*** Isn't it remarkable how God sprinkles such obvious signs along our journey? May we find strength and inspiration in surrendering ourselves to the higher power that guides us.

By embracing faith wholeheartedly, we gracefully navigate life's complexities, understanding that each step taken in reliance on God adds to the harmony of a purposeful and filled existence.

In the tapestry of life, the key to genuine happiness lies in placing God at the very center. Through this unpredictable journey, I've discovered that some of life's most profound revelations unfold as divine punchlines crafted by the Almighty Himself. Admittedly, Mom and Dad were happy when they heard that singing in church comes with a paycheck!

17

Facelift

'Lifting spirits and lives through collaborative partnerships'

In 2000, I co-founded and took the helm as inaugural President of the Professional Résumé Writing and Research Association *(PRWRA)*, spearheading a global coalition of career connoisseurs from 19 countries dedicated to setting the gold standard for résumé craftsmanship. Dr. Nelda Spinks, my technical writing professor from college was happy to step up as part of our PRWRA global advisory board. I love full-circle moments! Don't you?

Then, 9/11 came crashing in, sending everyone's career plans into a tailspin faster than anyone could say, *"Y2K panic."* Our worries about the millennium bug were just a tad premature – timing is everything!

While others were spiraling, I channeled my energy into something bigger than a career slump. Enter Volunteers for Careers – my mission was to provide free career services to 9/11 victims and families. In just two weeks, I rallied approximately 600 career professionals globally, creating a résumé revolution valued at more than $600,000. A collaboration orchestrated with Wendy Enelow and volunteers from PRWRA and the National Résumé Writers Association – talk about a résumé rescue mission!

"You will leave a mark long after you're gone. The careers industry touches every person around the world who holds a job."

REFLECTIONS OF COLLABORATIVE EFFORTS AFTER 9/11

Amidst the tragedy of 9/11, the world got cozier. Who could forget the Coldstream guard playing our anthem, Berlin waving American flags, or the naval rendezvous of the U.S. and German ships, proving that even in tragedy, the world becomes intimate and caring? During that time, the global "Cold War" became the "Warm Hug" War.

Every talented symphony has a conductor, section leaders, and individual musicians. When all work collaboratively, the creation of beautiful music can be enjoyed by multitudes of people.

Do you routinely collaborate with colleagues, or do you live a life distrusting your colleagues? The secret to successful collaboration is asking. People want to be part of something good that can make a positive difference.

18

Face Forward

'Leaning on your legacy for inspiration and forward thinking'

MY RETAIL LEGACY BEGAN IN THE 19TH CENTURY

I come from a long line of forward-thinking entrepreneurs and innovators from the mid-1800s. My great-great-grandfather Mervine Kahn was the "OG" entrepreneur of his day, turning a planned train ride to Beaumont into a detour love affair with Rayne, Louisiana.

March 1, 1884 – Mervine Kahn and his friend Michel Schmulen partnered up to create what would later become Mervine Kahn Company *(MKC)*. There were no fancy contracts, witnesses, lawyers, or fanfare, just a handshake and a dream. If that happened today, there would probably be an app for it, and they'd seal the deal with an emoji handshake. MKC was a retail destination, offering everything from buggies, groceries, clothing, appliances, and livery to the latest German-imported accordions because every Cajun needs a good accordion to spice up their grocery shopping experience.

And then, in 1963, grooming began for the passing of the retail torch to Dad. Our whole family had just moved from Midland, Texas to Lafayette, LA. Dad, a lawyer by trade, mastered the art of settling family disputes and legal affairs while running the store. There was legal drama but with more shopping carts.

The MKC motto was from a 19th-century playbook - *Money Saved Is Money Earned.* Moreover, Jeff Bezos, CEO of Amazon; the original retail Jedi was Mervine Kahn, and he didn't need drones to get the job done!

Cheers to the retail saga that kicked off with a train ride, a detour, and a sheet of lined tablet paper. The only tough decision associated with this family tale involved choosing between buggies and accordions for the inventory. For 106 years, MKC stood as a shining beacon of family-owned retail, creating success one historic sale at a time – a true legacy!

19

Face Your Partner

'Trusting God to send your perfect partner'

The cosmic comedy of love is where divine timing meets the awkward dance of introductions. Get ready for an inside look at my love life, where God took on the role of the ultimate matchmaker with a side dish of hilarity.

It was late in 2002, and I found myself living back home with my parents and navigating the choppy waters of a dissolving marriage while helping Dad, who was declining with advanced Lewy Body Dementia.

To rediscover myself, I embarked on a journey of self-care. Daily workouts? Check. Tanning salon appointments? Check. Confidence? Well, let's just say that was a work in progress.

Have you ever known someone who was a born matchmaker? Enter Sharee, a guardian cupid. Spotting my freshly single status, she decided to play Divine Matchmaker. I'm so grateful for Sharee. She approached me at church, whispering, *"Hey, I know the cutest guy. I've been praying about this. Can I give him your number?"* Well, who am I to refuse divine intervention? Plus, I'd seen Sharee's husband – the woman knows her cuteness metrics.

Fast forward a week, and Kenny James, the cute guy in question, rings me up. This sitcom could have been called *"ESharee.com."* God, the ultimate director, was weaving his comedic magic.

Add Tim Allis, my funny and ridiculously-talented friend to the mix. He drags me out for sushi, determined to break my spell of house arrest. Mid-sushi feast, Kenny calls. Ever the articulate one, I blurt out, *"Oh, is this Kenny? Hi!! I'm out having supper with a friend ... just a friend ... only a friend!"* Yes, I instantly became a walking definition of friend-zoning myself.

Post-Sushi, Tim delivers the classic platonic friend speech - a dramatic Shakespearean moment - *"Get over yourself and just give the guy a call tomorrow!"* Sage advice from a sushi philosopher.

The following morning, I drank a cup of courage and made the call. Kenny, cruising in his truck, graciously navigates my friend-zone fiasco. We found common ground in chocolate and old movies, planning a lemonade date at a burger joint the following day.

A seemingly simple soft drink date became a four-hour marathon of laughter, tears, and meaningful connection. And just like that, I'm floating on Cloud Nine – the VIP section of the cosmic comedy club.

Not content to let the spark between us stop, I invited him to meet my family for brunch the next day. Bold move? Perhaps. But when your life has turned into a love affair with sweatpants, you don't let the moment slip away. He agrees to brunch, and from that day forth, we're inseparable – a match made in stand-up comedy heaven.

Coincidences: Kenny and I were destined to collide in the grand scheme. Firstly, our parental units tied the knot on the same day, August 21, 1954 – talked about synchronized nuptials! Secondly, both dads proudly wore military stripes, answered to the moniker *"Sonny,"* and hailed from the East Coast. Thirdly, Kenny and I were poster children for fashionably late arrivals and, apparently, vertically challenged too – it's a small world, after all! Fourth, despite living in parallel universes *(okay, just two hours apart),* fate intervened when Kenny's parents RSVP'd yes to my brother's wedding. And believe me, there's a whole treasure trove of divine nudges that put us together.

Let's face it, Kenny and I were simply destined to rendezvous at that precise moment, primed and ready to embark on this beautiful life together.

So, there's my love story with a celestial twist. Sometimes, you need divine timing, a cupid friend, and a hearty dose of laughter to find the love of your life. Thanks, God, for the laughs, the love, and the lemonade dates!

20

Facials

'Continuing the quest as a lifelong learner can change your life'

While maneuvering the bustling streets of Los Angeles, I stumbled upon an ad promising a FREE facial. Now, who can resist the enticement of complimentary pampering, right? Little did I know that this would be my initiation into the dazzling world of Mary Kay – where pink isn't just a color; it's a lifestyle.

Picture me, a skeptic from a soap-and-water background, dipping my toe into the sea of *"pink"* for the first time. The Mary Kay Consultant worked her magic; suddenly, my face was a canvas of radiant pink perfection. I had discovered a secret to fabulousness.

Fast forward 20 years, and I found myself back in Lafayette, LA, collaborating with a Mary Kay Consultant who wasn't just any consultant but a sorority sister from college. She became my go-to makeup guru, transforming my wedding day into a flawless masterpiece on June 17, 2005.

After returning from our dreamy honeymoon, Kenny had a grand plan for me to retire so he could venture into the charter fishing industry. While he was all in, I wasn't thrilled about relocating to Florida and living surrounded by sun and sand. But fate had its comedic twist in store for us.

Days after our honeymoon bliss, Kenny and his new business partner jetted off to Miami with a quick jaunt to the Florida Keys, only to find themselves driving into the eye of a storm. Literally, while everyone else was fleeing the area, they were the lone car heading "in" to the Florida Keys. You guessed it: Hurricane Dennis was making a beeline their way, and the National Weather Service had sounded the evacuation alarm. Talk about a plot twist! Our plans took an abrupt U-turn, and I returned to my oilfield industry job.

Meanwhile, I had made a promise to a sorority sister to lend a hand at her Mary Kay event, and that's when my Mary Kay journey took a wild turn. I took the plunge on that rainy Friday night and became a Mary Kay Consultant. *(I am, after all, a retail gal at heart!)* I vividly recall coming home to tell Kenny about my $100 investment in this new venture, only to have him respond with, *"That's great! Can you help me change the sheets and clean up our house? There's a hurricane in the gulf, and my family's coming over from New Orleans tomorrow to escape the storm's path!"* And just like that, my Mary Kay pink bubble had just burst!

The next day, our tiny rent house transformed into a bustling refuge for quite the motley crew: nine adults *(one of whom was eight months pregnant),* two wise senior citizens, a spirited toddler, a cat, a dog, and yes, even a rabbit. Amidst the chaos, Hurricane Katrina's devastation became all too real, underscoring its place as one of the most catastrophic hurricanes in our nation's history. Just two hours west of New Orleans, our Cajundome *(a mere eight blocks from our rental)* served as a beacon of hope, offering shelter to more than 18,000 evacuees who couldn't find refuge in the overcrowded Superdome.

Fate had a twisted sense of humor, it seems. Less than three weeks later, on September 13th *(coincidentally, the anniversary of Mary Kay Cosmetics),* I was abruptly untethered from my full-time job. *(Thanks, Hurricane Katrina, for ushering in this unexpected twist!)* It felt less like happenstance and more like a divine stage cue orchestrated by God, propelling me again into the rosy realm of self-made ventures.

Sobbing, I called my Mary Kay Sales Director to share the news that I couldn't do Mary Kay because I needed to find another job. She said, *"Hallelujah! It's time for you to get your Mary Kay business going!"* Then Kenny chimed in, *"Do it! I believe in you!"* God had whispered, *"Try Mary Kay,"* and I thought, *"Why not?"*

To add insult to injury, Hurricane Rita decided to crash the party, making landfall near the Texas-Louisiana border as a feisty Category 3 hurricane. And while that might not sound like a big deal on its own, consider this: we still had displaced relatives floating around since Katrina. Now toss Rita into the mix, and suddenly, we were hosting another full-on hurricane party with a nephew and Kenny's parents crashing at our place for several days. Talk about a house bursting at the seams! And amid this chaos, there I was, trying to figure out how to "start up" a new Mary Kay business while every other consultant training me seemed to be gearing down in devastation!

But hey, I've never been one to shy away from a challenge. So instead of wallowing, I decided to flip the script. I mean, if I could survive the epic business challenges of the 1986 oil bust and the aftermath of 9/11, surely, I could handle a hurricane or two or three, right? With that newfound perspective, I plastered on a smile, rolled up my sleeves, and dove headfirst into my Mary Kay business. Because when life gives you lemons, or in this case, hurricanes – you whip up a batch of pink lemonade and make the best of it!

Oh boy, was it a world of pink dreams! With the business model of God First, Family Second, and Career Third, this was right where I needed to be. A substantial income stream, flexible schedules, and the joy of choosing my business partners - it was a beauty boss buffet. Mary Kay, you brilliant lady, changing lives for the better, one face at a time.

As an Image Coach, I've become a guru of all things pink and professional. I've trained countless colleagues in interviewing and doling out image makeovers like Mary Kay was sitting on my shoulder, coaching me through it all. My online conference support calls have transformed hundreds of sister beauty consultants into career promotion magnets.

In the Mary Kay *"pink bubble"* world, I've learned more than just the art of perfecting a smoky eye look. Goal setting, salary negotiations, onboarding wizardry – you name it. I've conquered each skill in a pink power suit. The company's accolades showered over me and made the journey even sweeter. I've honed skills in setting and achieving goals, negotiating salaries, onboarding teammates, interviewing customers, perfecting an elevator speech, managing time, presenting with success, and self-awareness. Mary Kay has changed my lifestyle, including multiple cars - trophies on wheels! Corporate didn't just hand me a starter kit; they gave me opportunities to take an entrepreneurial ride while consistently receiving prizes I didn't even know I needed. Winning the beauty consultant lottery is incredible!

Mary Kay hasn't just been a side hustle; it's been a game-changer. The recognition, financial reward, and leadership skills have elevated me to pink royalty on a national scale more than a dozen times. And in this magical land of makeup, we mentor and collaborate, creating a win-win outcome that's pink-tastic!

An Entrepreneurial Revelation: Years into my transformative Mary Kay journey, an epiphany hit me. The acronym for Mary Kay Cosmetics *(MKC)* echoed with profound familiarity – reminiscent of Mervine Kahn Company *(MKC)* – our cherished family department store in the heart of Rayne, Louisiana. This synchronicity became a powerful sign, weaving together the threads of my personal and professional life, igniting a renewed sense of purpose and inspiration on my remarkable path with Mary Kay.

When life rains on your parade, make sure your glam is hurricane-proof, and maybe, just maybe, consider joining the pink revolution. Because in the world of side hustles, nothing beats believing in the power of pink!

LaurieJJames.com, LLC: After passing the baton of my résumé writing and career coaching companies to trusted colleagues, I half-expected my passion to wane. But lo and behold, my reputation continued to sparkle like a 3-carat engagement ring. With a gentle nudge from my husband, I returned to solo practice, sans the expensive storefront jazz – opting instead for an intimate one-on-one résumé writing and career coaching symphony.

As technology wove its intricate web, I tuned in, guiding clients through the maze of virtual interviews, onboarding rituals, and the enigmatic art of personal branding.

Drawing from Mary Kay's experiences as both an Independent Beauty Consultant and Independent Sales Director, I infused a touch of glamour into the career sphere, transforming résumé writing into a glitzy, fashionable affair.

21

Face Books

'Drawing inspiration from unlikely places'

Lily Kahn, my wonderful cousin, defied expectations from day one; born with Cerebral Palsy but was raised by her determined parents to conquer the world as if it were her playground. Shipped off to an all-girls academy, she was to be treated like any other student despite her disability. And oh, how she thrived under the guise of normalcy, emerging from the educational gauntlet not just unscathed but empowered.

Post-academic life saw Lily stepping into her retail destiny, a true Kahn through and through, with her retail gene pulsating proudly. Lily's for Books sprang forth, a testament to her lineage and formidable spirit, charming patrons with razor-sharp wit and a heart as big as the Grand Canyon.

Enter Jim Morrow, smitten like a kitten in a creamery. His devotion to Lily was the stuff of legends, prompting even me to quip, "*I want to marry someone who loves me like you love Lily.*" Along came my own Jim – Kenny James, sharing a November 8th birthday and the surname James. It's as if the divine hand of fate decided to play cupid!

Beyond the hustle of her retail empire, Lily was a fairy godmother in disguise, sprinkling kindness like it was going out of style. She attended my Mary Kay debut, flipped the script, and joined my team to help me earn that coveted first free car and a promotion to Independent Sales Director.

One Thursday in November of 2014, Mom and I embarked on a mission to cheer up cousin Lily, who was feeling under the weather. Little did I know, ominous clouds of intuition were already looming. As fate would have it, Kenny and I left for a much-needed West Coast getaway, leaving behind a reluctant request for Mom to be our vigilant guardian over Lily's well-being.

Fast forward five days to a chilly afternoon on Alcatraz, the notorious island prison-turned-tourist attraction near San Francisco. Through the fog and gloom, my phone jolted me from the eerie ambiance with a solemn message. Lily had departed this world.

Stunned and disoriented, I sank onto a nearby bench, only to be confronted by Kenny, who confirmed the unthinkable with a single glance at his camera roll. There it was – a solitary Lily, defiantly blooming amidst the desolation of Alcatraz, a poignant symbol of her ethereal presence. When we returned from the vacation, we gathered family and friends to bid fond farewell befitting Lily's uncontrollable spirit. Through laughter and tears, and even a large bag of Hershey's kisses, we shared cherished memories to celebrate Lily's life and irrepressible love for chocolate and levity. She will always be remembered as an impactful member of our community and a pillar of generosity and heart.

In that bittersweet moment, as we all bid adieu to our beloved cousin and friend, we couldn't help but feel the embrace of her enduring legacy – a testament to the divine inspiration she embodied in life and beyond.

And leave it to Lily to plan her farewell with flair, requesting Ave Maria at her graveside. When I asked, *"Why Ave Maria? You're Jewish!"* she replied, *"That's okay. I'll be dead!"* She shrugged off religious boundaries with a witty retort, proving once again that even in death, she was the life of the party.

Let's all step on a stage with grace and gusto in life's grand scheme. Lily epitomized mischief, orchestrating moments of hilarity and happiness with unrivaled skill.

Here's to channeling our inner Lily, the director of delight, where every move is a graceful groove, and standing ovations are simply par for the course in the art of living.

22

Face Time

'Spending quality time by developing common interests leads to valuable lessons'

Aunt Barbara the lone ranger in Dad's sibling posse, also grew up in the humble town of Rayne, but her ambitions stretched far beyond its borders. Armed with a degree from the University of Miami, she spiked her flag in Houston, TX, where she served up a killer game as a PE Teacher and Volleyball Coach. Her heart was a perfect match with Hispanic students, diving for success past bureaucratic blockers like a seasoned volleyball libero.

In the game of life, Barbara was my steadfast setter, doling out affection like a well-placed serve and reserving a special place in her heart for Kenny, my ace in the hole. Our weekly powwows were marathon rallies of banter and bonding. Not a single milestone or festivity escaped her radar; she was the MVP of timely calls, always ensuring our celebrations began with her warm cheers.

Nana, her grandmother, and my legendary forebear became a recurring player in our chats. Through Barbara's stories, Nana's spirit was resurrected, along with the legend of her famed Caramel Cake – a treat steeped in sweet nostalgia. The icing on the cake *(pun intended)* was wearing Nana's century-old wedding gown at my nuptials, a miraculous fit that defied the odds and alterations.

In July 2017, Kenny and I undertook the arduous task of delving into Barbara's treasure trove posthumously. That summer-long effort revealed her true identity: a die-hard Astros fan and a meticulous keeper of memories. Her room was a shrine to Astros glory, including a prophetic baseball cap thumbtacked to her closet wall, foretelling their World Series championship later that year.

I couldn't help but imagine a divine negotiation, with God tempting Barbara to join the celestial team in exchange for an Astros victory. The call might have sounded like this, *"Come join me now, and the Astros will win the World Series!"* And in October 2017, the Astros finally claimed victory, sealing the deal on Barbara's heavenly negotiation!

Aunt Barbara was a curator of curiosities, a guardian of Astros relics, and a chronicler of our lives. Found among the memorabilia of baseball triumphs, she carefully preserved the artifacts of our marathon phone conversations, immortalizing my Mary Kay ambitions and vacation dreams that Kenny and I shared. Her steadfast encouragement and meticulous attention spoke volumes of her boundless love for Kenny and me.

In reflecting upon her well-lived life, I'm reminded that our bond transcended mere conversation – it was a lifeline of connection, advice, and understanding that only an aunt can provide.

Barbara's legacy serves as a poignant reminder to embrace life without regret, cherishing each moment as a gift to be savored.

23

Face The Nation

'Persuading efforts that changed the face of our nation'

In the early '60s, Mervine Jankower *(Dad)* embarked on a crazy Louisiana adventure that would make even the zaniest sitcoms seem tame. What I'm about to share is true because no one could make this up! Picture it: Lafayette, Louisiana, 1963, a town where the Republican Party was so exclusive they could host meetings in a telephone booth – a comedy classic.

Dad, a legal wizard, was in the middle of a political caper. The Lafayette Republicans, who could carpool in a VW Beetle, wanted to challenge a Louisiana gubernatorial election with a contender who had less chance of winning than a snowball in a bayou. Enter Charlton Lyons – Shreveport's answer to political prowess.

How do you drum up funds and excitement for a candidate in a sea of Democrats? Simple, find a celebrity! Armed with connections from Midland, Texas, Dad set his sights on Hollywood because nothing says political endorsement like a dash of Tinseltown. The target? Ronald Reagan. But this wasn't your average invite. A tenacious letter writer, Dad penned missives to Reagan, who was busy hosting *"Death Valley Days"* on TV. Reagan, being the gentleman he was, declined due to prior commitments. Enter George Murphy, the understudy for our political comedy – a suitable alternative, but Dad had a hunch Reagan was worth the wait.

Cue the cosmic gut punch. President John F. Kennedy was assassinated on November 22, 1963, just before the proposed Lafayette fundraiser in early January 19, 1964. Suddenly, political fundraisers seemed irrelevant. But undeterred by the somber tone, Reagan, with a fortuitous break in his schedule, agreed to the Lafayette engagement. A hastily organized, shoestring-budgeted fundraiser ensued – a political comedy on the rise.

Meanwhile, the superstitious Nancy (Reagan) spoke with her psychic, who told her not to let Reagan fly and insisted he take a train from California to Louisiana! He developed a slight cold at the last minute, and Nancy urged him to cancel the trip. But he wanted to fulfill the commitment while Nancy stayed in California with their young children.

Reagan rode cross-country for two exhausting days by train on the Sunset Limited to honor his promise to Dad and the growing conservative movement in Louisiana.

Picture this: a longer than two-day trek each way, illustrating a testament to Reagan's unwavering commitment to the conservative cause!

In the cozy confines of south Louisiana, Dad found himself in Reagan's orbit, thanks to those persuasive letters that lured the future President to the Bayou State. Soon after they met, Reagan gently asked him, *"May I call you Jan? And please just call me Ronnie!"* Because in the intimate world of Louisiana politics, everyone is on a first-name basis, even the future President of the United States.

Dad, now Reagan's personal chauffeur, whisked him to the Townhouse Motel. After all, what better venue for a future presidential pitstop than a motel?

Mom, Dad, and their tiny Republican crew welcomed Reagan to Lafayette with the pomp and circumstance usually reserved for a Mardi Gras parade. The Reagan speech was magnificent, leaving the audience utterly spellbound with both message and delivery. Picture it: a sold-out auditorium, $25 tickets *(equivalent to a small fortune today),* and Reagan at the helm of the political circus.

Post-fundraiser, Mom and Dad hosted Reagan in an intimate reception, where Crème de Menthe flowed freely, and cream cheese cookies disappeared in a flash.

As the soirée unfolded, a photographer suggested a group photo in the Jankower bedroom. With a mischievous twinkle, Mom remarked, *"Reagan was in my bedroom! Of course, there were 20 other people along with him!"*

As word spread about the political event, the Lake Charles Republicans, keen to jump on the bandwagon, begged Reagan to squeeze in an encore speech in their nearby city the following evening. Luckily, Reagan agreed.

The next day was filled with political activities. Since Mom was unable to join because my brother was a little under the weather and needed to be monitored, Dad escorted Ronnie to a local Lafayette TV interview, then, they grabbed lunch and got on the road to Lake Charles for that encore presentation.

While spending the entire day together, Dad got to have one-on-one personal conversations with Ronnie about conservatism, governmental philosophy, potential political aspirations, and life in general.

Then came the climactic moment in this epic adventure. An unforeseen train delay left Reagan potentially twiddling his thumbs in Lafayette.

With some quick thinking, Dad called Mom, the ever-hospitable hostess, before midnight, exclaiming, *"Put on the coffee pot! Ronnie's train has been delayed! I'm bringing him home to visit while he waits!"*

Mom fondly recalled, *"Reagan was just magnificent. He was VERY gracious, naturally poised, and extremely down to earth. Listening to him was a fantastic experience. We discussed conservatism and a multitude of other topics. Never in my entire life have five hours passed that quickly!"*

Picture it: the Jankower den, Reagan regaling mesmerizing tales of Hollywood. Mom was brewing coffee and serving cookies like Martha Stewart. Five hours flew by in a flash.

Alas, the train beckoned, and Dad, the political Uber driver, dropped Reagan at the station. Mom recalled the magical encounter in their den, *"It was the most fascinating conversation we ever had. He told us fantastic stories about Hollywood, Frank Sinatra, JFK, and many others."*

Reagan's *"thank you"* letter, dated February 4, 1964, praised Mom's bravery for staying up. Chuckling, she thought, *"Brave? Are you kidding? It was just magical, absolutely magical!"* Little did they know this incredible experience would be etched in political history.

Reagan was known as an actor, lobbyist, and a conservative speaker at this point in his career. However, this marked the first time he publicly endorsed an individual political candidate.

The cosmic joke? This seemingly small Louisiana escapade marked the genesis of Reagan's political journey. The impact rippled through history, culminating in Reagan's iconic *"A Time for Choosing"* speech at the 1964 Republican National Convention when he endorsed Presidential Candidate Barry Goldwater. Louisiana, with its phone booth Republicans and unpredictable fundraisers, unwittingly became a catalyst for change.

So, here's to Mom, Dad, and the tiny contingency of Republicans – the unsung heroes of a Louisiana comedy that altered the course of political history. Because sometimes, deep in a bayou, you find a political gem that sparkles like a swamp full of sequins.

One man's persistence to secure a well-known public figure for a Louisiana endorsement navigated this country's political future. We are all individually capable of making a positive impact. Just DO it!!

24

Showing My Real Face

'Figuring out your higher purpose in life is priceless'

If I could casually toss my financial worries, I'd be the caped crusader of volunteering, soaring in with my unique skills to rescue programs and people in need. Paychecks? Who needs them? I'd be swimming in *"God Dollars,"* the exclusive currency of fulfillment and purpose – a treasure far superior to Bitcoin, the stock market, an IRA, or even a stash of cash tucked under a mattress for safekeeping.

Nothing tickles my fancy more than utilizing my God-given skills and talents to assist others in achieving their dreams. This can take various forms; you can script your charitable payday with creativity!

Discover your true passion! It might be concealed within a hobby or something that just makes your heart sing. So, here's the lowdown: Are you a baby whisperer? Perhaps it's time to grace the hall of a Children's Hospital or a daycare center with your soothing presence. Do you excel at connecting with tweens and teens? Consider becoming the ultimate mentor at a nearby boys and girls club. If high school dynamics don't faze you, contact your local school for some volunteering gigs. Feeling more like a seasoned mentor who wants to shape our future? Lend a hand at a college or junior college – they could use your unique wisdom.

Suppose you've got a soft spot for elderly citizens. Assisted living facilities always look for individuals like you. They appreciate attention like cats appreciate tuna.

Is music your forte? Ponder joining the ensemble of your local community theatre or taking on an ushering role at a concert venue. Want to unleash your inner sports mania? Rack up volunteer hours at a youth sports camp – or attend a game and show kindness to others in your actions.

Regardless of where your inner passions reside, a starting point exists for the journey that could unveil your hidden superpower and propel it into a career capable of enduring the trials of time. Whether it's in the arts, sciences, or any other field, there's always a path waiting to be explored, leading you toward fulfilling your potential and realizing your dreams.

So, dare to embark on this journey, for within it lies the opportunity to transform your passions into a legacy that transcends generations.

Where do you begin? Explore local hangouts – churches, community groups, chambers of commerce – anywhere people gather for a noble cause. And naturally, a wealth of information is awaiting discovery on social media. Remember, the key to success is showing up. Or, as we say in south Louisiana, it's all about that GEAUX and SHEAUX!

Step away from your comfort zone, find your rhythm, and witness the transformation into your most extraordinary self. It's time to heed the call of destiny!

While others chase after that elusive dollar bill, I'd be out there amassing *"God Dollars."* They're priceless and in high demand, especially by yours truly.

Now, I'm throwing down the gauntlet. Dive into the quest for your higher purpose. Anticipate plot twists, laugh in the face of the unexpected, and, above all, relish the delightful adventure of life – because who needs financial stability when you've got a positive attitude, a pocketful of "God Dollars" and a hearty sense of humor!

Made in the USA
Middletown, DE
12 June 2024

55642826R00056